M000034208

~~Eleanor~~
~~Is an amazing~~
aunt - Love you
~~bunches!!~~
~~Love~~
~~Michele~~

Daring to Choose

Gaining Momentum

from your Darkest Days

ALOHA PUBLISHING

Michele de Reus

Daring to Choose
Gaining Momentum from Your Darkest Days

© 2013 by Michele de Reus

Print ISBN: 978-1-61206-051-4

Ebook ISBN: 978-1-61206-055-2

Publishing by Aloha Publishing

Cover Design: Cari Campbell of Cari Campbell Design and Amy Greensky of Greensky Graphics

Interior Book Design: Fusion Creative Works

Primary Editor: Kim Foster

All rights reserved. For use of any part of this publication, whether reproduced, transmitted in any form or by any means, electronic, mechanical, photocopying, recording, or otherwise, or stored in a retrieval system, without the prior consent of the publisher, is an infringement of copyright law and is forbidden. Some of the stories in this book are true to life, used with permission, and told as they happened. In these cases, names have been changed to protect the privacy of the individuals involved in the stories or scenarios. All other stories are composites of the lives of real people and any similarities to people you may know are purely coincidental.

The authors and Aloha Publishing shall have neither liability nor responsibility to any person or entity with respect to loss, damage or injury caused or alleged to be caused directly or indirectly by the information contained in this book. The information presented herein is in no way intended as a substitute for counseling and other forms of professional guidance. All Scripture quotations, unless otherwise noted, are taken from the New International Version Bible.

Published by

ALOHA
PUBLISHING

AlohaPublishing.com

Printed in the United States of America

"The unexamined life is not worth living."

Socrates

Dedication

This is dedicated to women who wonder if they will shine bright again.

You will!!

Contents

Introduction

Life has a way of opening new paths that are unexpected. Some paths are exciting and easy to travel, while others are painful and treacherous. It is as if you are on a lovely bike ride, and something hits you, pushing you over a ledge. You find yourself lying on rocky ground, not knowing if you have the strength to get back up. Your internal injuries are many: a bleeding heart, an abandoned soul, a broken and bruised ego. It would be so easy to shut your eyes and succumb to the pain and exhaustion you feel.

When I was pushed off a ledge with my life's first unexpected turn, I remembered the words of a song that I had often sung as a child in church. These words played over and over inside my throbbing head as I lay there, trying to find the courage to stand up.

Jesus loves me! This I know,
For the Bible tells me so.
Little ones to Him belong;
They are weak, but He is strong.
Yes, Jesus loves me!
Yes, Jesus loves me!
Yes, Jesus loves me!
The Bible tells me so.
(Anna B. Warner)

This little children's song gave me enough hope to figure out how to get off that rocky ground. I felt loved and comforted when I sang it. I knew that I was weak, and I knew that God had the strength to carry me. When I made the choice to let go and let God carry me through with His strength, it was a life-changing experience. You will experience how I witnessed God's love in extraordinary ways through ordinary people and their gifts as you read this book.

Your life is significant. No matter how much pain you feel at this moment or how tired you are, you can live fully, relying on God's strength to get you through the current situation so you can see brighter days.

Learn to get back up quickly, brush off the dirt, and get back on the bike to finish life's journey with purpose and joy. Listen to your heart and know that as you invite

God in, a wonderful transformation takes place. It is God's grace in action. God gives it to you as a gift, and all you have to do is choose to accept it. You will gain the necessary momentum to ride again with joy, peace, and everlasting love.

Joyfully riding on,

Michele

"Then they cried to the Lord in their trouble,
and He saved them from their distress.
He sent forth His word and healed them;
He rescued them from the grave."

Psalm 107:19-20

Choose You

Created in God's Image and Worth Fighting For

Bad things happen to good people. It is unfair. Life can give you days that are really terrible. In fact, they are awful. There are so many ways we can look at life. We can definitely see the disturbing things life throws at us and wonder why we should even get out of bed because it isn't going to get better.

At 27, life hadn't thrown me a lot of punches, and the punches it had thrown me seemed to be pretty manageable. What I hadn't expected was the love of my life, my husband, Ian, telling me one thing and doing another. Instead of facing the discontentment he was experiencing in our marriage, he chose to step out of the marriage and continue to deny his actions. Today, I know he was not bad or evil; he was hurting, while trying to find his own way to live authentically with who he was and what he believed to be true for him. It was sad that the way he chose to figure himself out was very hurtful to me.

At one time or another, we will experience something that hurts our soul to the core. For each of us, it could be something very different. It could be betrayal, the loss of a loved one, the diagnosis of cancer, or the loss of a job or a big business venture.

These feelings can knock us for a loop and sometimes they can knock us *flat*! Flat down and we don't know how to get back up. At first, we ask the question, "Why me?" The next step is daring to choose you, choosing to heal from the inside out to gain the strength to face any obstacle that you face, no matter how hard it is. It takes an act of faith to make the small steps, trusting that it is going to get us to a place that is peaceful and joyful. It allows us to have a deeper understanding of ourselves and a deeper compassion for others who are hurting as well.

If we were made in the image of God, then we aren't made of junk, even though we may feel we're being treated like junk. There are outside forces that want to tell us lies about ourselves: we are not worthy, not loveable, and we are not valued. Those forces feed on our insecurities, our weaknesses, and our doubts.

Self-doubt is an ugly thing. It is like an invasive weed that, if watered, grows quickly. In my case, it was a matter of learning the skill to eradicate the weeds of self-doubt that were choking my self-esteem and causing me to shut down. Focusing on God, the true source of love and light, is the first step in weeding our garden (our soul). God says that it is yours if you ask. Every day was a conscious choice to step towards a healthier me and a step towards true love—the love of God. Paul states in Romans,

> "For Your sake we are being put to death all day long; we were considered as sheep to be slaughtered. But in all these things we overwhelmingly conquer through Him who loved us. For I am convinced that neither death, nor life, nor angels, nor principalities, nor things present, nor things to come, nor powers, nor height, nor depth, nor any other created thing, will be able to separate us from the love of God, which is in Jesus Christ our Lord." (Romans 8:36-39 NASB)

How does that resonate with you? *Nothing* can separate us from the love of God. That includes a whole laundry list of things. Even my husband falling out of love with me did not separate me from God's love. If nothing can separate us, can't we conclude that we are worthy of love? That our life is of value and that God has a purpose for our lives? This revelation was huge for me, and I hope it is *huge* for you too. Our feelings will go up and down, in and out, and will contort all through the day. God's love is constant, immense, and forever! God chose you and created you. It is time to choose you and regain your strength and health to be the person God created you to be.

I ask you to take this promise, and no matter if you really believe it, take steps in faith to learn about it and gain momentum from the dark days you are currently facing. It is a daily choice. Possibly, it will be an hourly choice to move through the pain. I assure you that it will get better, and the pain will become less daily, weekly, and then will be manageable because you will be transformed, living in God's pure love, forgiveness, and grace.

Each chapter is set up for you to:

Contemplate your story. Reflect upon your current situation. Write it all down. Journaling is the first step in facing it head on and taking the daring, bold step to work through the hurt to a state of contentment and confidence.

Imagine a better story. What would the story look like if you could imagine a better story? What feelings and actions would support being loving to yourself and to others, without you feeling like a doormat, hateful, revengeful, or arrogant whether or not the story changes? Take a moment to write it down. You might have to take a day or two to consider what that better story would look like.

Example: I want to be able to go through this painful situation without feeling unworthy and without hurting so much. I want to feel secure in God's love no matter what happens in my marriage. I want to be joyful and not be a doormat. I want to learn how to express my voice without being angry. I want to listen, to understand, and articulate to be understood.

In your words: Write your response.

Invite God in. Invite God into the story to change hearts—to change your heart. He will love and support you through this story so you can have peace through the situation. You will learn to respond lovingly without being a doormat or revengeful. God will guide and strengthen you to health and vitality.

Example: Dear God, You know this situation intricately. You love each and every one of us. I'm hurting and I give You that hurt. Protect my heart as You guide me through this as gracefully as I can get through it. When hurtful words are thrown out, allow them to bounce off me. Hold my tongue tight so that I don't say hurtful things I may regret later. Give me strength and courage to be the mother, wife, and woman You want me to be. May I feel Your love and Your peace throughout this day. I give this situation over to You and ask that You heal me, transform my heart, and guide me. Amen.

In your words:

Declare your value. If God's love is pure, then we can be confident in that love. We can state our request as if it has already happened. I will give you examples and will ask you to write your own. At first, this may be very uncomfortable. Take a step towards trusting that the exercise will be inspiring and healing. Give it time and you will quickly see that your attitude and demeanor will change when you make these declarations throughout the day.

Example: I am strong, confident, and loved. My strength is from God, and I have the endurance to get through this situation confidently while being at peace. I articulately express myself while my heart is protected from words and actions that can hurt me. I am safe in God's arms.

Take a moment to write your value statement right now. Say it in the present tense as if it is already a part of who you are. Say it out loud so you can hear yourself. If you find yourself saying it without conviction, try some different cadences so that you say it with conviction. Say it like you feel it is already who you are!

Your declaration:

"Have I not commanded you?
Be strong and courageous.
Do not be terrified;
do not be discouraged,
for the Lord your God
will be with you wherever you go."

Joshua 1:9

Choose Momentum

Getting Unstuck

I can't move. What do I do next? The thought of facing the world just doesn't seem appealing at all. I don't want to be inundated with questions or with advice to do this and that. Where is God through all of this?

If I listen down deep inside and admit my feelings, I am scared. I am angry. I'm hurt more than I have ever hurt before. I feel foolish, believing the answers that I heard when I asked the questions, "Is there something that we need to talk about? Is there someone else?" My gut was telling me something was wrong in my marriage, and now after several months, the facts surface. I am flat! Flattened down emotionally, mentally, and a lot of the times, physically. What is my next step? How do I get out of this dark hole that seems to be enveloping and swallowing me up? I'm questioning life itself.

These were true feelings of a time that visited me long ago. It feels like another lifetime, as if another person lived through it—not the me of today. The little hope that I had back then was enough to cling to and make the necessary steps to work through the pain. Today, I'm no longer haunted by those dark questions. I have a joyful and full life, even when I have bad days and have to work through painful decisions. How do we get through those days that stop us in our tracks? How do we keep moving before becoming resentful, bitter people?

I met a woman a few months back, and she said to me, "I feel betrayed." She was young and just diagnosed with a rare cancer. She felt like her body didn't hold up to its end of the bargain when she had taken great care of herself. She wanted to see her young children grow old, and now that was in question.

I pondered the choice of words she used: "I feel betrayed." It is interesting how the human condition can sense betrayal in such a variety of ways. We face betrayal by our bodies when they grow old. Some may face betrayal in a marriage. Others feel betrayed when a great business venture fails after investing thousands, possibly millions, of dollars and hours of hard work. Betray is defined in Merriam-Webster's as: "to lead astray; to deliver to an enemy by treachery; or to fail or desert, especially in time of need."

Wow—to deliver to an enemy. Those are powerful words. No wonder I didn't feel like moving or getting out of bed, or this woman didn't feel like facing cancer, or a dear friend who lost his business wouldn't answer his phone for months and rarely left his house.

Are you wondering what the next steps are to get through the challenge you are currently battling and to feel hopeful for the future? I want to encourage you that it is *well worth* getting through the pain. It is well worth taking the steps to climb up out of the dark pit, no matter how small the light is at the surface. It is not easy. It takes courage and you have it!

God made a promise to you, to me—to everyone.

> "For I know the plans I have for you," declares the Lord, "plans to prosper you and not to harm you, plans to give you hope and a future" (Jeremiah 29:11).

Today, you might be asking, "Why me?" But what if, instead, you asked, "What needs to shift in order for me to gain momentum in a healthy direction?" The true source of love can get you on a path of healing. That is pretty cool.

Think about the list below. What healthy action can you implement today that would move you forward, making you feel better right now? Highlight that and begin implementing it immediately. Each day add another one from the list. Implement as many of these ideas that gets you up, providing you with encouragement to tackle and address the bigger issue.

- Find a verse from the Bible, a quote, or even a song that resonates strength and possibility to you—avoid ones that make you feel melancholy and sad.

- Contact your family doctor to get a physical evaluation, including an assessment of your mental health and sleep. Please note that sometimes it is hard to know if normal reactions to difficult life events have moved to clinical depression, which warrants treatment by a professional. Take a moment to read *Recognize the Signs of Depression*, by Dean Anderson, located in the Tool section at the end of the book.

- Read, read, read. Read books about what you are going through. Get educated on the subject matter that you are tackling. Read works that inspire and motivate you, not works that further darken your day.

- Workout. If the thought of going to the gym is unappealing, then go on a walk along a beautiful path or take a hike in the hills. Start out with 10 to 15 minutes and then add 5 more minutes each week until you are getting exercise three to four times a week for a minimum of 20 minutes. Really look at the beauty around you. Look at the flowers, water, hills, ocean—the vegetation around you. Look at how unique everything is. Enjoy the smallest thing and savor it. Think about how intricately made you are.

- Join forces with trusted friends who are compassionate and encouraging. Stay away from friends who are draining and want to wallow in self-pity with you. There should be a healthy mix of venting, listening, and focusing on something outside of what you are going through. Remember, it is not your friends' job to fix this for you. This is something that God will help you get through.

- Interview and choose a great counselor who can give you an assessment and a plan of attack. Look for one who seeks to find healthy ways of assisting you to get out of the "hole." Give the counselor two to three visits before you decide if he or she is a good fit.

- Once every two weeks, do something special just for you. Maybe it is having a massage, a pedicure, or a weekend getaway. Maybe it is going out to a nice dinner.

- Consider eliminating alcohol while you are moving through this obstacle.

- Feed your body healthy, nutritious food. Fast food and sweets should be eaten in moderation.

- Consider doing something new that you have always wanted to learn, and meet a new friend while doing it.

- Once the cloud lifts, do something small for other people. Try to make their day either by giving them a compliment, baking them cookies, or bringing them coffee. Getting out of yourself is very helpful and up-lifting as you experience helping someone else and brightening their day.

- Be grateful when something unexpected happens in your day that makes you feel good. God will work in powerful and fun ways to show you that you are valued and loved and that you can find hope again. Make it a habit to be thankful when you notice these little kind and compassionate acts.

Some days you will take three steps forward and other days you will take two steps back. That is a total movement forward of *one step*. When I was in that dark place, I had a couple of daily mantras that I held close to my heart. I wrote them down and kept them in my pocket so I could read them when the dark, gloomy thoughts wanted to be my companions for the day.

"Be still and know that I am God" (Psalm 46:10a).

"Never will I leave you; never will I forsake you" (Hebrews 13:5b).

Imagine a better story. Take a moment. How would you like to envision your current story? Is this a realistic expectation—one that can happen by making some changes? Is it something that would take a miracle such as healing cancer? Whatever it is, write it down here.

Example: Each day I begin to breathe easier and easier. I continue to take care of myself and I feel stronger. The next doctor's visit, I hear the medical staff say that my cancer is in remission. The next doctor's visit after that, I hear that my lungs look like they are healing themselves.

In your words:

Invite God in. Take this time to invite God into your situation in your own way. There is no right or wrong way. You are God's creation. John 16:24 states, "Until now you have not asked for anything in my name. Ask and you will receive, and your joy will be complete."

Example: Dear God, I'm hurting and angry. All I can think of is how it deeply hurts and asking why. I cry out to you, oh God, to comfort me and to give me peace. Give me hope for the future and give me the courage to make the steps needed to feel whole again. You, God, are more powerful than anything that I am going through. Please restore my soul and give me Your power and strength to get through. Amen.

This step is your statement where you have asked God and you have received it. Even though the answer might not have happened yet, state it as it has. Set the intention that you have received and you are grateful.

Example: I am whole and complete in God who created me. I am loved by the Creator of the universe, and I am confidently moving forward with God's strength and love that resides in me.

It's your turn to write your "Declaration of Value." Use the "I am" statement as if it is already so. Along the side of the declaration, write a verse or quote that supports that statement and resonates with your soul. Use a recipe card and carry it with you, reading it several times throughout the day!

"Bearing with one another,
and forgiving one another,
whoever has a complaint against anyone,
just as the Lord forgave you,
so also should you."

Colossians 3:13 (NASB)

Choose Forgiveness

There is Freedom in Doing

Forgiveness. What a simple yet complicated word. We need to forgive in order to heal from within. The act of forgiveness can be very hard, and it often does not happen overnight. It can be so difficult that it seems like months may go by and lack of forgiveness still lingers in our soul, hardening our hearts. Or we push back the memories into the far recesses of our mind, hoping to escape their haunting shadows in our lives, only to be reminded that they are still there, needing to be dealt with.

To forgive is not condoning the person's actions, whether they did it intentionally or not. The act of forgiveness is really healing from the inside out, allowing us to feel free from any chains that are tugging at us. It frees us to love again, trust again and frees us from bitterness and resentment. So, the action of another person has caused a reaction in ourselves that can hurt us even more than the original action against us. Are we really willing to allow unforgiveness to become bigger and more damaging to ourselves than the original action against us? Please consider that statement.

In 1988, my brother-in-law's eldest daughter, Andrea (a child from his first marriage), was 19 years old. She had just graduated from Capital High School in Boise, Idaho, and moved to Sacramento, California, to begin college and live with her mother. She was a vibrant, loving young lady, full of vitality and youthfulness. Andrea had many friends and she was so excited for the future. Her life was cut very short when she left her job one day. Working at a high-security dispatching office, she left to either study for school or go hang out with friends. What ensued has only been speculated by the police, but we do know that she never came home that evening, and she was unrecognizable when she was found later. She had been molested and beaten to death—a horrific, violent crime.

It was a tragic act of violence that hit our family hard.

Jennifer, Andrea's sister, who was closest to her, was in the eighth grade at the time. I was amazed at how well she forgave and moved on healthfully. Jennifer is 44 years old now, and I am still amazed at how well she went through that irreproachable event in her life. She realized that she was not the assailant's judge. He would be judged by God, and she did not believe that was her job. Though she missed her sister and hated seeing her mother, father, and young sister in pain, she knew that she wanted to be free from bitterness and resentment. During that time, she really evaluated her spiritual walk and what God meant to her.

With my own situation, I did not want to forgive Ian. I was hurt by his actions and was angry that I felt forced to divorce him because he wanted out. I no longer wanted to stay in a marriage where I questioned my husband's love and commitment. Forgiveness was a choice for me, and it is a choice for you. I don't think that forgiveness can be done alone. It is a supernatural occurrence when we make the choice to forgive and ask God to help us forgive. It is also looking to find if a "victimhood" mentality is still present and giving that over to God to heal that area of our life. It is like peeling back an onion layer by layer. Sometimes, those layers can be painful, causing our eyes to burn in the revelation of the new layer.

Contemplate your story. As I peeled back each layer, the bitterness went away, and I was filled with an immense amount of joy and contentment. Bitterness was replaced with love and compassion. Like life itself, it is a process.

Imagine a better story.

Example: I ask questions to clarify and get understanding. I am free of resentment and forgive easily. I release whatever has offended me to God, the ultimate higher power and referee. I state clearly my expectations and answer truthfully when questions are asked of me. If I do not know the answers, then I let that person know and contemplate them. I get back with them to let them know my answers. I state my answers with confidence. If I need to be flexible and listen to another point of view, I do so. I'm coachable and will ask for forgiveness when I have done something wrong. I will forgive quickly just as I would want to be forgiven quickly.

In your words:

Invite God in.

Example: Dear God, I hurt. I'm angry and I want to be free from the resentment I feel for someone I loved so deeply. I release all these feelings to You and ask You to teach me to forgive this person and forgive myself. Give me the strength to do it and protect my broken heart. I thank you in advance for giving me a heart that forgives, loves, and desires to seek Your will for my life. Amen!

In your words:

Declare your value.

Example: I am loved and complete in God. I freely love, forgive, and protect my heart and soul in a healthy manner. I have healthy boundaries and am confident to love and trust again. I attract people who are honest, healthy, and respectful. I ask for forgiveness when I have wronged someone right when it happens. I also quickly forgive others just as I would want them to quickly forgive me.

Your declaration:

I learned a forgiveness visualization exercise from one of my spiritual coaches, Tammi Baliszewski, PhD, author of *Manifesting Love, From the Inside Out.* She outlines how "this exercise will help you sever the connections to those who have hurt you." She gave me permission to share the exercise, with minor modifications here so you can use it too. Use it as often as you need to work through and gain total forgiveness. This exercise can be done whatever your spiritual beliefs are. It is the act of acknowledging the feelings, sharing the feelings, letting go, and loving yourself to the next step of greater growth and healing.

(See Tools: Forgiveness Visualization on page 143.)

"For God did not give us
a spirit of timidity,
but a spirit of power,
of love and of self-discipline."

2 Timothy 1:7

Choose Love

The Other Mother

Ian and I had been divorced for less than a year, and the days we traded our four-year-old son, Cole, were uncomfortable and awkward. For a few hours after being dropped off, Cole liked to spend one-on-one time with me. We did a variety of activities during these hours, and this day we were playing Candy Land, a popular board game.

Cole looked up at me, and with a glimmer in his eyes he proudly said, "Dad and Lisa are getting married." "Oh?" I stammered, "Tha-a-a-t's cool." I found my heart beating fast, my face getting warm, and my stomach knotting up. I'm sure my reaction would have been suspicious to another adult, but my four-year-old didn't seem to notice.

The man who had been my husband was going to marry again, and Lisa was going to be my son's stepmother.

Lisa, Ian's girlfriend, had been around since Ian and I had separated the year before. We had some interaction with one another, but communication was mainly with Ian, which was still tense and uneasy. Today, I faced this new revelation. The divorce still hurt. I still felt unsettled being a single woman and mother. How was I going to accept this new fact?

After their marriage, Lisa began establishing her role as their family matriarch, and more times than not, it rubbed me the wrong way. She had a certain way of doing things, and I had my way of doing things. We were asking Cole to be adaptable to both, which I felt was unfair to Cole. I felt threatened as Cole's "real" mother. Time and time again, my conversations with Ian and Lisa dissolved into "he said/she said" scenarios. I felt that I had to give up my dreams of how I wanted motherhood to look and it scared me.

After a heated discussion with Ian and Lisa, I remember getting down on my knees while the tears streamed down my face and crying to God, why did this have to be so hard? Why did I feel like the enemy when Ian was the one who wanted out? Why did we question everything with each other when we both knew we had similar value systems? Why did he trust her opinion over mine?

I prayed for strength and, above all, for wisdom. After I was spent, totally exhausted, venting these questions to God, I began asking, what did I want for Cole? Did I want him to see an angry mother? Did I want him to feel like he had to pick sides? How did I want him to see his parents communicate with each other? I knew that Lisa and I communicated much better than Ian and I did. She didn't have the deeply grooved recordings that Ian and I had established over the years. She heard me differently than he did. She heard me as a mother and a woman, not necessarily as Ian's ex-wife.

My ultimate desire was for Cole to see a parenting relationship that was respectful, cooperative, and supportive to his well-being, so he could feel loved by all of us—and that included Lisa. Lisa's nature genuinely seemed to care for Cole. She was teaching him, holding him accountable, and loving him. At the time, she didn't have kids of her own, and I saw that her expectations were high. Lisa established a home for Cole where he had two other sets of loving grandparents. I asked myself, "Isn't that a good thing?"

I had to make a choice. I asked God to heal me, to teach me to forgive, and for wisdom to see this situation differently. Proverbs 3:5–6 became my mantra: "Trust in the Lord with all your heart and lean not on your own understanding; in all your ways acknowledge Him and He will make your paths straight."

As I released control of how the relationship "had" to look, the more I saw a beautiful relationship forming between Cole and Lisa. It was happening without sacrificing my relationship with Cole. Both could develop simultaneously. Our parenting unit was moving forward, more smoothly than before. It was still a little sticky and sometimes stalled on the muddy trail. In time, Lisa and I began to trust one another whether we agreed or not. We really tried to listen by staying on the topic at hand.

I remember a conversation we had after she had her twins. She was extremely fatigued as she began establishing a schedule for them. Our conversation was getting heated and my voice started cracking.

She asked, "Are you crying?" "Yes," I said. "Why?" she wondered. "I remember how tired I was when Cole was first born and from one mother to another, I think you are amazing. I can't imagine how fatigued you are as a mother of twins. You seem to be holding it together so well." At that moment, we connected as mothers, not as Lisa and Michele with our individual agendas, but at a deeper understanding of the sacrifices mothers give innately because they love their kids.

Today, I can say that I *participate* in a working parental relationship, and it contains three people—all raising *our* son. Cole is loved by a big family which includes one father, two mothers and a large extended family. He trusts that we are united in looking after his well-being. The three of us collaborate, using our unique gifts to foster his growth as a young man. The other woman was not the enemy. Instead, God helped me see Lisa as a blessing in Cole's upbringing. I'm grateful that Lisa accepted the role as stepmom and that she battled her way through the journey with me, along with God's grace, to get where we are today.

Contemplate your story. Is there something in your life that is not sitting well with you and yet it is out of your hands—something that is out of your control and yet deeply hurts when you think about? Take a moment and write what "it" is.

Imagine a better story. Are you able to imagine a better story where everyone is served to their greater good? For example, in the story above, it isn't really about me and my hurt feelings, it's really about my son feeling loved by his entire family—even if that family is defined differently than how I originally viewed it. So, in your story, should your focus be on someone else rather than your-self? What do you need to do to shift your focus? Take a moment to imagine a better story that's better for every-body—not just you.

In your words:

Invite God in. Take a moment and write your prayer and meditation. Remember that God hears you wherever you are. What a beautiful expression of love when the Creator of love can meet you right where you are and love you right where you are. How cool is that?

Example: God, thank you for loving me when I am un-lovable. I lift up all that are involved in this current situation and ask that you work it out for the highest good for all that are concerned. Heal my heart and shield it from any additional darts. Allow those darts to hit a wall that is not of me. Give me a peace that only comes from You. Give me a heart of love and compassion so that I am present and available for my responsibilities and to my son. Thank you for the answer to this prayer.

In your words:

Declare your value. Take a moment to write down your declaration, stating it daily until it is a part of you. Revisit it when you see your actions are not matching the words.

Example: I am compassionate and strong. I am a vehicle of love and my heart receives everything that is from God and of God. I focus on my responsibilities and excel at everything I set my hand to. I give and receive graciously!

Your declaration:

"For I know the plans I have for you,
declares the Lord,
plans to prosper you and not to harm you,
plans to give you hope and a future."

Jeremiah 29:11

Choose Trust

A Trusted Friend

Wow, I had just gotten off the phone with Ian and was not quite sure what to think. He informed me that Lisa had made an appointment for us to see a counselor because she thought Cole, a fourth grader at the time, had a suppressed anger problem that needed to be addressed. Cole had been playing cops and robbers with a sixth grade student and some tough words were thrown out in an angry expression. Ian shared it with Lisa, and she made the call to set up the counseling appointment. Ian wanted to let me know about the appointment.

Wasn't this a normal thing that was said when kids played cops and robbers? I thought. My mind started racing, and I wasn't sure that Cole "really" had an anger problem that was coming out during this cops and robbers game. However, I didn't want to be naïve to think that the divorce hadn't left a mark on him, and I wanted to remain open. I agreed to meet them at the counseling appointment.

My stomach was in knots. I was entering a new arena with Ian and Lisa. We were far from having a civilized parenting arrangement at the time. I felt really alone and wanted support in some way. I didn't want to go into that counseling appointment with the feeling it was me against them, nor feeling that I didn't have an opinion to express, yet wanting that opinion to be heard. How could I support myself during this counseling appointment, asking the needed questions and best supporting my son? What could I do to strengthen my voice as Cole's mother because I wasn't feeling that my voice was being heard from Ian?

As the week unfolded, I offered up my fear of being the outsider to God and prayed for wisdom in this situation. Questions emerged.

- What could I do to support my voice at the counseling appointment?

- Who could I take to the appointment to support Cole and me, and be an asset to this counseling appointment?

- Who would be objective in this situation?

My first thought was to take a family member; however, I didn't want them to coddle me or be angry with Ian and Lisa. This would have made me anxious, not able to focus on the topic that was being addressed. My thoughts went to Grace. She was a dear friend. She had a boy Cole's age, and she understood his age group. She was a person who looked objectively at life events and was not an alarmist. She would also support me and my voice and would not be intimidated. She would be appropriate and would ask questions to help draw out answers and support.

As I shared the situation with Grace, laying out my fears and asking for her support and her opinion, she was responsive and agreed to attend. I wasn't sure how the appointment was going to unfold and she understood that. The counselor wanted to see all of us individually, and I was set up to be last. When Lisa and Ian came out, they were more frustrated than when they went in, and there was no explanation about what had happened in their meetings. All I knew was that when Ian left his appointment, he was angry and very frustrated. My stomach was feeling tense and I didn't know what to expect at all when it was time for my appointment.

Since I was getting more anxious, I decided to go in alone and asked Grace to wait in the lobby. When I came out, it was wonderful to see my friend there to greet me.

I was able to debrief with her, bounce off ideas with her, and get her perspective. I felt prepared and supported to go back and discuss everything with Ian, knowing that he and Lisa would have had time to talk about their individual sessions.

Contemplate your story. Are you in a situation right now where you might need some support from a trusted friend, relative, or counselor? List three to five names of people you feel you can trust. To the right of each name, answer the following questions:

- Will they add a level of support that is appropriate for the situation?

- Will they support your voice while remaining diplomatic?

- Will they be confident and stand up for you if your voice is not being heard and you are struggling emotionally to communicate clearly?

- Do they know how to ask questions that draw out answers?

- Are they calm and resilient?

- Will they keep your confidence and remain confidential?

Example: Everyone in the scenario has had time to review their appointment and evaluate the overall framework of what is going on. We collaborate creatively on the next steps, putting together an action plan that works well for everyone and addresses our son's needs first and foremost. It produces the objective we are seeking in a healthy and supportive manner. We treat everyone involved with respect and compassion.

In your words:

Invite God in. Spend some time in prayer lifting each person up to God and asking for the support and guidance only God can give. Ask if there is a person who can be your advocate in the situation. Pray for God's blessing. Listen for the answer. If you don't get affirmation to invite a friend, trust that God will provide you the strength needed to get through the situation.

"Do not be anxious about anything, but in everything, by prayer and petition, with thanksgiving, present your requests to God. And the peace of God, which transcends all understanding, will guard your hearts and your minds in Christ Jesus" (Phil. 4:6–7).

Example: Thank you, Lord, for strength. Thank You for the peace that replaces my anxiousness about this situation. I will hand over my anxiousness to You, knowing that You know my request, and I can thank You in advance for the peace and understanding You will give me. Thank You for guarding my heart and mind through Your Son, Jesus.

In your words:

Declare your value.

Example: I am confident that I am supported in this situation, and I desire to be wise and know the will of God. I am loved, supported, and wise. I am a good listener and ask appropriate questions. I will not take things personally.

Your declaration:

"Do not forsake wisdom,
and she will protect you;
love her, and she will watch over you."

Proverbs 4:6

Choose Healthy Boundaries

Supportive and Loving

Stella was an incredible mother, friend, and woman. She had been divorced for over two years and was now married to a wonderful man. She was the mother of three children. Her daughter, Amy, was born between her two sons. Amy was always close to both of her parents, and during the divorce, she pulled away from Stella, saying some really nasty and hurtful things to her mother.

Stella regrouped time after time, trying different approaches to reach out to her daughter, while working to regain her own strength and constitution. It was hard. Sometimes it worked; sometimes it didn't. Stella felt guilty because she thought that maybe she deserved some of this backlash because the divorce was her idea. However, she made a conscious choice to leave the marriage because abuse didn't stop as it should. There came a time when she was done with the mental abuse that was directed at her year after year in her marriage.

As she got stronger, she began setting healthier boundaries, which conflicted sometimes with her daughter's thoughts about how her mother should behave to her. Wasn't she entitled to berate her mother? It wasn't always easy. Stella tried creative approaches, setting up environments so that she could enjoy her daughter, letting her know she was loved and supported, but also having boundaries that would not allow for the daughter to be verbally abusive toward her mother.

Amy participated in girls' lacrosse, and she was one of the star players. Stella called another dear friend and me and asked if we would join her to watch Amy. Her hope was by having us there, that the interaction with her daughter would be more positive. Amy wouldn't feel like she could be mean to her mother, and she would feel supported and loved because there was more than her mother watching her. We agreed wholeheartedly, knowing what she wanted to create, and we loved watching Amy.

The game was on a beautiful spring day. When the game ended, with Amy hailed as one of the most valuable players of the game, the three of us approached her on the field to give her high fives and praises. Amy smiled. Stella felt supported and the three of us walked away from Amy, knowing that we had created the environment to accomplish Stella's objective. Friends are here to help support healthy choices for ourselves—to regain healthy boundaries that support and heal.

Today, Stella and Amy are continuing to find their way to build a healthy and loving mother/daughter relationship. Stella has had to let a lot go, and it has been hard. As Amy matures, she is reaching out to her mother more, and they are able to have interactions that are mutually supportive and healthy in nature.

Contemplate your story. How are your relationships? Are you giving people permission to be abusive towards you? Maybe you cannot completely remove yourself from these people because you work with them, co-parent, or they're your own family, as is in this case.

Imagine a better story.

Example: I'm going to identify a few friends who will support me in creating a beautiful scenario where my daughter feels loved and I feel respected. The scene provides a healthy environment to have a positive exchange of words, hugs, and smiles. I will walk away feeling joyful

and full of love for my daughter, knowing that I supported her. I will be thankful that I created a healthy boundary for myself and was supported by loving friends who
care for my and my daughter's well-being.

In your words:

Invite God in.

Example: Thank you, God, that I have the courage to
strengthen my boundaries and still show love to others.
Thank you for the wisdom to invite supportive friends to
help me set up a beautiful and loving scene to show my
daughter she is loved while being respectful to myself.
Thank you for the healing that has occurred and for the

full healing that will come. Thank you for loving all the people involved and giving me the courage and wisdom to handle this matter in a healthy manner. Amen.

In your words:

Declare your value.

Example: I treat myself with respect while loving the important people in my life healthfully and passionately. I treat others the way I want to be treated. I can create healthy environments that are respectful and loving for everyone involved. I ask for support from friends and family who are loving and trustworthy.

Your declaration:

"He will cover you with his feathers,

and under his wings you will find refuge;
his faithfulness will be your shield
and rampart."

Psalm 91:4

Choose Healthy Boundaries

Tested and Confirmed

A few months ago, Don, a man whom I've shared an 11-year friendship with, and I decided our relationship had run its course. I thought I enjoyed his company; however, after spending time with him, I would find myself feeling drained and lousy. Our communication was really stifled. We never understood each other, no matter how hard we tried to explain our side. Because we liked many of the same things, I began accepting the way I felt was just something that was a part of this particular friendship.

As I was working on myself and getting clearer with my direction, I began seeing that our time together was robbing both of us of an uplifting and enriching friendship. I have always valued my time with friends and family, and I was not valuing our time together. I kept my distance and chose to meet up with him for coffee every few months. We tried talking about it because we both loved God, yet the differences and the uncomfortable feelings remained.

A girlfriend told me to sever the friendship—that it was not "worth my time". That seemed so heartless and unkind to me. I couldn't do that. He was a man whom God loved and he had countless gifts–one being that he is a good steward of people, helping them, and befriending them in times of need.

The last time we got together and had coffee, Don shared his discontentment with our friendship, saying that he felt it was one-sided. I knew I had been distant. I knew that it was important for me to keep the healthy boundary, and now it was being challenged. What was I going to do? We tried discussing it, sharing our own perspective of the situation, and I felt that it didn't get us anywhere further in understanding each other. He didn't understand my perspective. I didn't understand his perspective.

In my opinion, it was time to let go and say thank you for the times we shared and to wish each other the best. I didn't feel any remorse or sorrow. I wasn't angry. I just knew that the friendship had run its course. I had never experienced this before in a friendship. I walked away from this meeting, wishing him the best and knowing that I had really taken care of myself in a very healthy and supportive way and had given all that I could have in this friendship.

As we set healthy boundaries for ourselves, they can feel a little awkward at first. I didn't hate this man. On the contrary, I cared for him and wanted the best for him. I shared time and a friendship with him for many years. We talked about our families and helped one another when we needed it. I wanted him to have joy, love, and contentment in his life.

As life often does, my boundary was tested. I was working in a coffee shop when Don quickly came in, heading to the restrooms. I looked up from what I was doing. We saw each other. Don curtly said, "hi" and I said, "hi" back. I wondered what would happen when he exited from the restrooms. Would he come out, come up to me, and would we catch up a bit? I thought about what I would do if I was the one coming in and saw him sitting here. I realized I would be comfortable coming up to him, saying "hi" and asking how he was doing. If I was busy, I would be able to come up to him, shake his hand, and let him know that I wanted to say "hi" and that I had to run out because I was busy.

I don't think that is necessarily how Don felt because as he came out of the restrooms, he walked in front of my table, without turning his head, walked out the door, got in his car, and drove off. I thought about the friendship of the past, and I could have possibly made some assumptions about where he might be at that moment. The thing is, I didn't need to do that. Our boundaries are here to keep us healthy. I'm not responsible in making it better for the other person. I can be kind, loving, and genuinely present to love another person. I can lift up that other person in prayer, knowing that God loves them and wants the best for them as God wants the best for me.

Contemplate your story. My boundary was tested that day and it was confirmed that the right choice had been made.

Imagine a better story.

Example: I can set healthy boundaries at the beginning when they are easily established and still love and receive graciously. I am consistent in maintaining them.

In your words:

Invite God in.

Example: Dear God, thank you for this past friendship. I thank you for the healing you have done inside me and the peace I feel right now. Thank you that I am not feeling like I have to "fix it" and that I can give it to you immediately. I pray for Don and lift him up to you. I pray that he is at peace. Thank you for loving us right where we are at any given moment. I pray for wisdom, humility, and the ability to love as you love others. Amen.

In your words:

Declare your value.

Example: I am a confident woman, knowing my self-confidence is not rooted in other people's reactions to me. It is rooted in God's strength. I know that I was created in God's image. I am humble, peaceful, and love people right where they are.

Your declaration:

"I can do everything through Him who gives me strength."

Philippians 4:13

Choose Health

Through Thick and Thin,
Our Bodies Are Ours

As women, it is easy to want to please the men in our lives. We can contort and shape ourselves to be what we think people want us to be. And if this goes on for a long time, we can begin to wonder what our true, authentic self is.

Melinda was one of my best friends, and we were in high school track together. It was during the winter of our first year of high school. We were in the gym working out with the entire track team, including the cute junior and senior guys. We were working out hard and doing everything the coach called for us to do. All of a sudden, we hear a coach yell at us, "de Reus and Smith, drop 10."

We couldn't believe our ears. I looked down to the floor, fearful of letting the track guys see the tears that were forming in my eyes. The coach was yelling in front of everyone for us to drop 10 pounds? In front of the cute junior and senior guys—really? We were mortified. (Both of us were thin and did not have weight problems.)

When I was 24 and sitting at dinner with my fiancé, he asked if he could divorce me if I got large. He was totally serious. (Understand that I did not have a weight problem back then either.) I couldn't believe what I was hearing. It reminded me of when I heard the coaches yelling at practice. That question was foreshadowing of things to come for me. After the divorce and a bike accident, I allowed the weight to creep on, thinking it was protecting me from men who were only focused on weight and outside beauty.

Melinda's story was a bit different. She went to college on a track scholarship. What she saw around her were young women, binging and purging to prevent weight gain. They would do this the night before a track competition, asking their bodies to perform again at a level without the necessary fuel to perform at the collegiate level. She found herself joining in and quickly realized that it wasn't going to lead her in any direction but in a negative one. She chose not to compete the next year, forgo her track scholarship, and focus on academics.

Both of us battled outside perceptions of what our weight should be and struggled with our self-esteem. We were both athletes, healthy and vibrant women. Fortunately, we both have healthier body images now than we did back then, in spite of what was said to us.

When we are working through difficult times in our lives, it is tempting to take the easy way out and eat quickly prepared foods or fast food. We don't have the energy to work out, so we don't, which further perpetuates feeling bad about ourselves. If we are taking a car on a long road trip, we would make sure it is filled up with good quality fuel, had an oil change, enough water in the radiator, and all the spark plugs were firing correctly. We want the car to handle well on the long road trip. When we deal with a challenge in our lives, we have to give our bodies the same type of treatment as we would in making sure our car is ready for the long drive.

Contemplate your life. Take a moment and consider how you are treating your body. Do you have some weight to lose in order to move easier and feel better? How about your workout routine? Are you getting out and being active several times a week?

It's not about wishing our bodies were different and punishing ourselves. It's about accepting our bodies where they are right now, being grateful for them, and moving towards optimum health. Then we can begin or continue creating the bodies we want with a healthy, active lifestyle that keeps us vibrant and strong to tackle what life gives us. As our bodies become or continue to get stronger, so does our mental health.

Take a moment and write down what you can do differently to support healthy eating and a healthy activity schedule. Maybe it is buying organic or fresh whole foods, preparing the food yourself, getting into a program (such as Weight Watchers), or joining a support group. If you think you are eating for emotional reasons, consider reading the book, *Shrink Yourself*, by Roger Gould, MD. This is an amazing book that steps you through the emotional bonds of eating to learning new, healthier patterns of eating and addressing issues that are being masked by overeating.

> "The wise woman builds her house, but the foolish pulls it down with her hands"
> (Proverbs 14:1 NKJV).

Imagine a better story. What does your activity level look like? Does this area need improvement? What can you do to support yourself or motivate yourself? Consider asking a friend to work out with you. Consider learning a new activity, such as aerobics, indoor cycling, a boot camp class, or training with the Leukemia and

Lymphoma Society's Team in Training for a half or full marathon.

Think of the possibilities that support and lift you to a new level of activity. I decided to teach aerobic classes again because it forced me to the gym, and I gain pleasure in helping others. I taught in my earlier twenties and was struggling to make it to the gym consistently. I could always talk myself out of it because I had clients to work with or a friend would call to do something else.

Once I decided that was what I wanted to do, I met a woman who owned a gym, told her my idea, and she asked me to call her exercise coordinator. The pieces began to fall into place. I started out with subbing, and today I teach four indoor cycling classes a week and have just hired a personal trainer to work on my upper body and core strength. It would have been easy for me to say I wasn't fit enough to teach. Instead, I invited in a solution to bring that back into my life that was fresh and exciting. That solution isn't for everyone. Find your solution and believe that it will be attainable.

What would you like to try to increase your fitness level? Write down some ideas and write down what steps you are going to take to make it happen.

Example: This month, I'm going to try out Zumba™, Boot Fit™, indoor cycling and a yoga class. After trying one, I'm going to add two of these into my weekly schedule two times a week. I am going to get on the Leukemia and Lymphoma Team in Training website and see if they have something going on in my area. I will call them and set up an appointment to find out what they are all about and whether I would like to train with them while raising funds to help others. I will finish my first half/whole marathon by the end of next year.

In your words:

Invite God in.

Example: God, you know the struggle I have with overeating and eating quickly. I ask for Your loving guidance through this addiction to put me on a path of health, wellness, and recovery. Help me to eat to fuel my body and support its organs so it is an efficient machine, running well and smoothly. I thank you for the strong body I have. Thank you that I live in America where food is plentiful. Open the doors so that I will find an activity that I enjoy, which allows me to train my body for endurance and strength. Surround me with encouraging people and put a strong wall around me so that when someone says something that is hurtful or isn't supportive, it will bounce off me.

In your words:

Declare your value.

Example: I am strong, lean, and weigh my ideal weight. I work out with confidence and complete my workouts.

I listen to my body when it tells me to rest and refuel. I feed my body with good nutrition and eat the amount that is appropriate to maintain my ideal weight. Thank you, thank you. I am so grateful for my strong, healthy, and beautiful body.

Your declaration:

(Note: As your fitness level increases, I encourage you to come back and revisit the reflection, your "Invite God In" statements and declarations. Tweak them to take the next step towards optimum health.)

"So I say to you, ask,
and it will be given to you;
seek, and you will find; knock,
and it will be opened to you."

Matthew 7:7 (NASB)

Choose to Ask and Receive

Be Ready to Be Surprised

Really? The break up happened and it was rather uneventful. In fact, it wasn't a breakup; it was an understanding that we were great friends and that the relationship was not developing any more than that.

I'd come a long way since my divorce where I felt an urgency to seek approval from the man I was seeing. Sometimes, we try to contort ourselves to be the person someone else wants us to be. It is freeing to really look for the source of our approval to be from the main *source*. That source is God. Whatever your spiritual walk is, God's love is power. It is unconditional and it is healing. There is grace and hope in turning our heads and hearts to that source, asking for God's approval. That approval is a gift and all we have to do is graciously accept that gift. There are no conditions, no hurdles to jump, no contortions involved. Isn't that cool?

We begin to heal from the inside as we love ourselves and accept that we are a gift from God. When we graciously accept that gift, we will see the power of God work mightily in our lives. There is no need to be afraid because we are loved. We can walk bravely and confidently. In fact, we can give over every aspect of our lives to God.

It has taken me awhile to learn this. I laugh when remembering how God answered a prayer of mine. I was sitting in a book shop on a Sunday and wishing there was someone of the opposite sex in my life to spend the day with. I gave my feelings over to God and asked, "Dear God, you know how I am feeling, and I'm not bound by those feelings. I give them over to you and I look forward to how you are going to answer my loneliness." I really didn't have an expectation. I thought the feeling would go away.

God answered my prayer in such a humorous way that day. About an hour later, a dear friend walked in the door, and we were surprised to see one another. We had been friends for a long time and knew each other when we had both been married. We had kept in touch through the years periodically, but we hadn't seen each other for awhile. We laughed and shared stories. Whatever I needed that day, it was given to me in a very special way. All I had to do was ask. It was a special and fun time with an old friend.

In the past, if I wanted to have something happen, I pushed to try and create it. If I felt like meeting up with a friend, I would begin dialing until a friend could meet. It rarely felt good when I did that. Think about how you are showing up in the world. Are you experiencing things that are uncomfortable? Are you pushing when you should be waiting? What can you do when you have to wait? That is when same-sex friendships are so important. Go to a movie, get coffee, or invite a girlfriend to be an exercise partner.

Contemplate your story. As you learn to wait, God will enrich your life more than you could have imagined. It probably won't look like you expect. What if it shows up better than what you expected? That is pretty cool, right? We've all heard the term *ego* right? Well, when our ego gets in the way, it is really *edging God out*. When we invite God in and ask for comfort when we are lonely, there is an expectation to see how that is going to be answered. We can ask for anything and everything.

- A healthy new friendship

- Our bills to be paid

- Improved cash flow

- Peace in the day when we feel anxious

- A night out

- Improved work relationship with a coworker

- The ability to learn a new hobby

Imagine a better story.

Example: When I am lonely, frustrated, needing wisdom, I will immediately lift my request up to God. I will be expectant, knowing that my prayer will be answered. I will be ready to receive the answer knowing that it will be better than what I imagine and it will be perfect for the situation—just the thing that is needed. I will have a grateful heart and say thanks out loud when I see the answer given by God!

In your words:

Invite God in.

Example: Dear God, I'm lonely (frustrated, mad, anxious—put whatever feeling you are feeling in here) and give this feeling over to you. I look forward to how you will answer my prayer requesting that I don't feel lonely (frustrated, mad, anxious, etc.) today. Please take away these uncomfortable feelings and fill me with a sense of wholeness and contentment. Give me the encouragement and clear direction to address my responsibilities. I thank you in advance for your answer. Amen.

In your words:

Declare your value.

Example: I surrender all things over to God. I am confident that I will receive answers that surpass my expectations, and they will be perfect for my situation. I am at peace, knowing that all things have been surrendered to God who loves me.

Your declaration:

"But those who hope in the Lord
will renew their strength.
They will soar on wings like eagles;
they will run and not grow weary,
they will walk and not be faint."

Isaiah 40:31

Choose to Ask and Receive

Renewed and Inspired

The winter morning was cold, and my cat jumped into bed wanting to get under the warm covers with me. I was of the same opinion; nestling in bed sounded better than heading out to teach a 5 a.m. indoor cycling class. The alarm chimed loudly for the third time. I had to face getting up this cold morning and venturing outside whether I liked it or not.

I jumped out of bed, bustling to put on my cycling clothes and headed out to a cold SUV. Realizing that I had been grumbling the whole time, I took a deep breath and began praying, "Dear God, give me peace and encouragement this morning. I am tired, discouraged and am feeling overly anxious. Clear my mind so that I can encourage and give others a great workout this morning. Amen."

I could see the members setting up their bikes, even though the room was dark. There was a lovely couple who were "regulars," Tom and Sara, who came early to get a one-mile run in on the treadmill before venturing into the cycling room. I enjoyed talking with them, listening to their wonderful stories in their Scottish accents. After getting his bike set up, Tom walked over to the three front fans to make sure they were set up, circulating the air well in the room.

"Tom, thank you so much for doing that. That is so kind of you," I said. Tom turned towards me and said, "You're welcome. By the way, I know you prefer the yellow LeMond bike over the Schwinn, so I switched it out for you. I'm not quite sure the settings you like." I could feel a sense of warmth in my face and my eyes tearing up. "Uh…uh…Tom that was so nice of you. You don't have to do that." Sara laughed and said, "Tom loves helping out. He knows the bikes that each of the instructors like and makes sure that they are set up for you before you get here."

What an amazing, heartfelt gesture! I felt so honored that this man took the time out of his early morning to make sure I had the bike that I liked to ride so I was comfortable when I was teaching. It wasn't the easiest thing to switch the bikes around in the room because the bikes were compact in the room. I'm sure he had no idea how much this one gesture touched me this particular morning. Driving to the gym, I had been "in my head" and now this man's kind gesture was encouraging and uplifting.

Are you feeling discouraged? Do you have to do something today that you do not want to do and know you have to? I encourage you to give it over to God. Open yourself up to His grace and love. You just might be surprised how He answers your prayer to show you that you are loved and valued.

Contemplate your story. God showed me a wonderful thing that morning and in a way that I was least expecting it.

Imagine a better story.

Example: Immediately when I am disgruntled, I will give my bad mood over to God. I will take four deep long breaths. I will say two things for which I am grateful.

"Do everything without complaining or arguing" (Philippians 2:14).

In your words:

Invite God in.

Example: Dear Lord, I thank you for this day You have given me to do Your work, and I give You the praise. I give You the discouragement that I feel today, and I ask You to replace it with encouragement and joy. Give me the energy to teach and meet the needs of each of the members today, giving them a great workout. I look forward to seeing how You answer my prayer, and I will give You the praise. Amen!

In your words:

Declare your value.

Example: I am energetic and strong to get through to-day's tasks and responsibilities. I am encouraging to others and am passionate in what I do. I do everything to the best of my ability.

Your declaration:

"Trust in the Lord with all your heart
and do not lean on your own understanding;
in all your ways acknowledge Him,
and He will make your paths straight."

Proverbs 3:5-6

Choose to Ask and Receive

A Healing Tool That Frees You from the Past

There was a time when a picture from the past would come to my mind or when I heard a familiar song on the radio, I would feel the same level of pain and sadness as if I was actually reliving it. For example, I remember the time when my husband no longer looked at me lovingly and longingly. Instead, when he looked at me, I interpreted it as a look of disgust and vacancy. I didn't know at the time that he had already exited out of the marriage. Being a person who is kinesthetic and visual, I didn't know what to do with this information. Without healthy boundaries, I found myself taking those looks personally and engraving them in my brain unintentionally and in an unproductive manner. In doing that, I experienced over and over again the hurtful and sad feelings that made my stomach go into my throat, choking off my words and making me feel suffocated. Sometimes these feelings caused me to be unproductive for several hours.

After sharing this with my counselor, he decided to try a technique on me called Eye Movement Desensitization and Reprocessing, or EMDR, a form of psychotherapy developed by Francine Shapiro, PhD. This technique resolves the development of trauma-related disorders caused by exposure to distressing, traumatizing, or negative life events. According to Shapiro's theory, "when a traumatic or distressing experience occurs, it may overwhelm usual cognitive and neurological coping mechanisms. The memory and associated stimuli of the event are inadequately processed and dysfunctionally stored in an isolated memory network."

Shapiro continues, "The goal of EMDR therapy is to process these distressing memories, reducing their lingering influence and allowing clients to develop more adaptive coping mechanisms."

This technique was used successfully with the victims of the 1995 Oklahoma bombing incident. Initially, talk therapy was used to help the victims get through the trauma and was later found to be ineffective for several of them. When EMDR was used, a large portion of the victims were able to successfully go back to work and function again.[1]

The method is simple to participate in and includes visual, auditory, and kinesthetic stimuli. Within two sessions, the visual memory of the events that were creating the distressing emotional responses no longer created the same level of response that I found disabling. I could envision the past memory without my stomach going into knots or hear a song and not feel like I was about to cry. It was amazing! I felt that I had broken through a tremendous wall and was able to move forward with clarity and confidence. EMDR is a gentle tool that is safe, non-evasive, and completely cool in my opinion.

Note: Check out www.emdr.com, where you can learn more about this amazing technique, and read Shapiro's new book, *Getting Past Your Past*.

Contemplate your story. In your story, what tools may help you break through and speed up the healing process? It might be EMDR or it could be meeting with a counselor or minister for a few counseling sessions. Maybe you don't know the tool that would help you break through. Ask God to reveal a tool that will assist you in healing.

---

1 Francine Shapiro, PhD, EMDR: The Breakthrough "Eye Movement" Therapy for Overcoming Anxiety, Stress, and Trauma. (New York: Basic Books, Member of the Perseus Book Group, 1997).

Imagine a better story.

Example: I can remember hurtful past memories without feeling the emotional body response. I can go through my day, picturing the past pictures and be grateful that they are only memories and I am strong, healed and free of bitterness and sadness.

In your words:

Invite God in.

Example: Dear God, thank you for the professional licensed clinician you brought into my life, who shared EMDR with me and freed me from hurtful memories.

I am healed from their stranglehold, and I am forever grateful.

or

Dear God, I'm stuck and I don't know how to get unstuck. Open the doors so that I may learn of a book, a technique, or a professional who can help me through this brick wall that I am facing. I am coachable, God, and I want to break through and be healed. Amen.

In your words:

Declare your value.

Example: My eyes are open to see possible effective tools that will help me break through this wall. I am coachable. I am free from the thing that binds me.

Your declaration:

"If we confess our sins, He is faithful and just and will forgive us our sins and purify us from all unrighteousness."

1 John 1:9

Choose Grace

A Wise Man, a Wiser God

The funeral was small. The father of my childhood friend had passed away the previous week. When I called to see if there was anything I could do, my friend talked about how her father, Bill, had prepared his funeral—all of it except the flowers. It had made it easier on her, allowing her to focus on the really important things. The priest leading the service was his nephew, and I was surprised at how wonderfully intimate, comfortable, and funny the service was. I sat back and heard the stories, remembering when my friend and I had been teenagers and were eating apples in Bill's front yard.

Dusk was upon us. I heard a car making the turn a few houses down, and said, "Watch this. I bet I can hit the car with this apple core."

I listened really hard, trying to time my throw just right...
wait...wait...wait...throw...*splat*! I did it! The core hit
the front window with accuracy. The car screeched to a
halt, and Colleen and I panicked. "Oh, no." What do
we do now? A frightened glance passed between the two
of us as we bolted to the back yard and slid through the
back door into the living room. We sat on the couch and
acted like nothing had just happened.

Colleen's dad said, "What's up girls?" "Uh, uh, uh...w-w-
we were out front and I tossed my apple core behind my
shoulder and it hit a car!" I couldn't believe it. I had just
lied. I had lied to my friend's dad. To a man I respected. I
continued, "They stopped their car and it looks like they
are coming back." Colleen and I were still breathing hard
when we heard the knock on the door. We froze.

Bill got up and walked to the door. He answered it and
there stood the driver of the car. I don't remember the
face of the driver. What I do remember is that Bill apologized for us. He said that he knew his daughter and her
friend very well, and they never would have done something like this on purpose. There wasn't any damage, so
the incident ended about as quickly as it had begun.

Even though I laugh about it now, the experience made
quite an impression on me. I felt so remorseful about
lying to this man, and I also saw what he believed about

me was true, that this was not typical of my character. I knew it wasn't my typical nature either. I had just tried to be a little different—a little daring for this one moment—by showing off to my friend. Here I was playing the victim role when I purposefully threw that apple to see if I could hit the car. I timed it perfectly, and I was not admitting what I had intentionally set out to do. It was a mistake. I knew it and I didn't want to own up to it.

When we make unwise, hasty decisions that are out of our character, such as when I lied to Bill, doesn't God forgive us as quickly as Bill forgave me? Bill apologized for us. It was over; we could move on. We didn't need to continue sharing the story with him—pleading our case. It was over. That is true with things that happen now as I am an adult. Justifying our position is not always the healthiest thing to do. Sometimes, it is simply knowing that we are forgiven, so we need to forgive ourselves and move forward. No need for drama…no need to tell the story again and again. Get on and move forward.

Contemplate your story. Take a moment to reflect on your life right now. Is there drama going on? What can you do to cease the drama? Take a moment to consider your options. Some ideas to consider are

- Do you need to ask for forgiveness?

- Refrain from sharing the story to someone and someone else? Zip your lips?

- Ask God for the power to end the drama. You might find that you will get so bored with hearing the story again that you will change the subject.

Take a moment to write down the ideas that you want to do to *gain momentum* to eliminate the drama.

Imagine a better story.

Example: You go through a painful ordeal, and instead of sharing it with many people, you may share it with one or two of your closest friends. You will gain their perspective so you can evaluate your next step. It is not to bad mouth or cast blame on someone else and avoid ownership of your responsibility. The better story ceases when gossip starts.

In your words:

Invite God in.

Example: God, thank You for Your love and grace. I'm loved deeply and completely by You. Your power is greater than the drama I am involved in at work (put your "drama" in here). I ask for Your power to remove the drama. Forgive me for my involvement in the drama, and I ask for You to give me the strength, courage, and skills to move forward and out of this. Thank You in advance for Your healing power and grace.

In your words:

Declare your value.

Example: I state the facts and my opinion without adding exaggeration. I commit to interact with genuine concern and compassion and only tell the story when necessary and to whom it is appropriate.

Note: State it daily until it is a part of you. Revisit it when you see your actions are not matching the words.

Your declaration:

"Devote yourselves to prayer,
being watchful and thankful."

Colossians 4:2

Choose Gratitude

Be Thankful for What Is and Is To Come

How is your gratitude? Do you believe that there is not much to be grateful for lately? The happiness that you once felt seems to be veiled by an opaque curtain, being elusive far from your reach? During these times, making a conscious choice to be grateful is an act of will that will benefit you. The more you focus on the things around you that you can blame, grumble, or complain about, the more you will see only the negative and the bad things that are happening all around you.

What if you chose to be grateful for the things that are beautiful in your life? They are all around you. Sometimes, it is just the fact that you got out of the bed and got ready to face the day that you can be grateful for today. If being grateful is hard right now for you, I challenge you to think about the little things that you can express gratitude for.

- Breathing easily

- Having a roof over your head

- Having a person in your life whom you can call friend

- Having a family who loves you

- Giving birth to a healthy child

- Having a body that works

- Living in a country that has freedom of speech and religion

- Having a job

- Having a dog that is happy to see you

- Experiencing sunny days that wrap warmth around you

When you make the choice to be grateful, you train your mind to see the good in all things happening around you. When I say this, I think about the four seasons. I have always loved living in a place where there are four distinct seasons. As I get bored with one season, the new season pushes the old out the door.

Think about it. Winter replenishes our water supply, kills off insects, signals hibernation to many animals, and gives us skiing! Spring comes in and gives us more rain to replenish the water supply, while vegetation and flowers begin to bloom; summer brings the warmth of the sun, playing in water, bike riding, summer vacation; and fall, the changing of leaves, coolness in the air, and harvest season. Each season has its downsides, and without each one, it is hard for our world to sustain itself. We need to be grateful for each one.

Contemplate your story. Take a moment to think about five things for which you can be grateful. At least two of those things should be things about yourself, such as your smile, your intellect, being creative, friendly, calm, and resilient, etc.

Example:

- I can make people feel comfortable.

- There are four seasons.

- My health is amazing.

- I see the glass as half full.

- I have a son whom I love and who loves me.

Imagine a better story.

Example: I choose to look at life from a state of love. I want to believe the best in people, and I'm thankful that I can express myself and listen to others. I choose to see the beauty in other people and situations before jumping to conclusions. I choose to ask clarifying questions and avoid making unfounded assumptions.

In your words:

Invite God in.

Example: Thank you, God, for this day. Thank you that I am able to get out of bed, take a shower, and face the day, knowing that I can get through the day in Your strength. I choose to be grateful today. I choose to be thankful. Remind me that because You created everything, I can find beauty in all that is around me. Thank you for the barista that gets my coffee in the morning and smiles at me. May I meet that person's smile with my own. Thank you that I can smile. Thank you that I can express myself. There is so much to be grateful for, and I ask you to open my eyes that I might see the beauty all around me and *in* other people, so I can begin to appreciate that beauty. Amen.

In your words:

Declare your value.

Example: I am grateful to be alive and breathing. I am grateful that when I smile others smile back. I'm grateful to hear a child laugh. I'm grateful that today when a car cut me off, I laughed instead of cursing.

Your declaration:

"For nothing is impossible with God."

Luke 1:37

Choose to Thrive

Shining Bright Once Again

Recently, I attended a presentation given by a woman named Linda. She is well known in our local market as an inspirational and motivational leader. I had never heard her leadership presentation before and was really impressed in how motivating and inspiring she was to the crowd, which was made up of 92 percent woman. The 8 percent of men in the room were also inspired as they gave their super woman poses when they got up to make an announcement.

As I listened to her talk, I thought about how far I had come in 20 years. Life doesn't necessarily get easier. When we choose to get better, life seems easier because we have the coping skills to ride the waves of challenges and jump over the hurdles it gives us. We have become better! This woman in front of me today was sharing that life was not easy for her early on either. Her mother died when she was a toddler, her father had multiple marriages after that, and she was kicked out of her home as a teenager, returned, and kicked out again at the age of 15 years old. She could have ended up being one of the statistics we have heard about: a child runaway getting into drugs or other self-sabotaging tactics. Instead, this woman, at an early age, chose to go to school and graduate. No one was in the audience celebrating her accomplishment.

Today, she is a vibrant woman, celebrating a successful 21-year marriage, being a mother of two healthy children, and inspiring women and men all over the valley to be the best they can be. She believed in herself, when the people closest to her didn't believe in her and she behaved as if she believed in herself. I hope that the stories shared in this book propel you forward to believe in yourself, knowing first and foremost that God loves you, and you are meant to shine brightly.

You can get better even though life doesn't get easier. You can thrive and feel of value in life as you participate in it, giving and receiving graciously, abundantly and enthusiastically. As we work on the inside, we gain the strength to be conquerors of life, cheerleaders for others who need to be lifted up, and creative stewards of our environment.

I am a true believer in the concept that as you are learning new skills, you might have to fake it until you make it. Amy Cuddy, a social psychologist speaking at a Ted Talks conference, says, "If you feel like you shouldn't be somewhere: fake it. Do it not until you make it—but until you become it." I love that! As we focus on building new skills, a way of becoming better than we were, there will be many times when we will feel uncomfortable and have a bit of an out-of-body experience. With faith, hard work, and practice, these new skills and mindsets will become part of us.

My life is no longer about being a resentful and angry, divorced, single mother. I'm a vibrant woman of life with many talents that range from being a woman, a child of God, a mother, a coach, a real estate agent, an adventurer, an indoor cycle instructor, a daughter, a sister, a small business owner, an advocate of women business professionals, a skier, and now an author. I am strong, giving, loving, loyal, honest, and I strive every day to be better than the day before.

Today is your day! It is your day to shine and envision how you want to show up in the world. You have learned to choose you! With that you have learned how to choose forgiveness, love, trust, and gratitude for everything that comes your way, and you will be able to handle it. If it doesn't feel like that, then choose to trust God to get you through it. God will provide the people, the community, and the environment to show us the direction to get there.

I'm so excited to hear how the stories inspire you and give you hope. I would love your feedback. Your personal story is important. Feel free to send your stories to me. Your stories can be sent to:

DaringtoChoose@gmail.com

Joyfully riding on,

Michele

Declarations at a Glance

I am strong, confident, and loved. My strength is from God, and I have the endurance to get through this situation confidently while being at peace. I articulately express myself while my heart is protected from words and actions that can hurt me. I am safe in God's arms.

...

I am whole and complete in God who created me. I am loved by the Creator of the universe, and I am confidently moving forward with God's strength and love that reside in me.

...

I am loved and complete in God. I freely love, forgive, and protect my heart and soul in a healthy manner. I have healthy boundaries and am confident to love and trust again. I attract people who are honest, healthy, and respectful. I ask for forgiveness when I have wronged someone right when it happens. I also quickly forgive others, just as I would want them to quickly forgive me.

...

I am compassionate and strong. I am a vehicle of love and my heart receives everything that is from God and of God. I focus on my responsibilities and excel at everything I set my hand to. I give and receive graciously!

...

I am confident that I am supported in this situation and I desire to be wise and know the will of God. I am loved and supported. I am a good listener and ask appropriate questions. I will not take things personally.

...

I treat myself with respect while loving the important people in my life healthfully and passionately. I treat others the way I want to be treated. I can create healthy environments that are respectful and loving for everyone involved. I ask for support from friends and family who are loving and trustworthy.

...

I am a confident woman, knowing my self-confidence is not rooted in other people's reactions to me. It is rooted in God's strength. I know that I was created in God's image. I am humble, peaceful, and love people right where they are.

...

I am strong, lean, and weigh my ideal weight. I work out with confidence and complete my workouts. I listen to my body when it tells me to rest and refuel. I feed my body with good nutrition and eat the amount that is appropriate to maintain my ideal weight. Thank you, thank you. I am so grateful for my strong, healthy, and beautiful body.

...

I surrender all things over to God. I am confident that I will receive answers that surpass my expectations, and they will be perfect for my situation. I am at peace, knowing that all things have been surrendered to God who loves me.

...

I am energetic and strong to get through today's tasks and responsibilities. I am encouraging to others and am passionate in what I do. I do everything to the best of my ability.

My eyes are open to see possible effective tools that will help me break through this wall. I am coachable. I am free from the thing that binds me.

···

I state the facts and my opinion without adding exaggeration. I commit to interact with genuine concern and compassion and only tell the story when necessary and to whom it is appropriate.

···

I am grateful to be alive and breathing. I am grateful that when I smile others smile back. I'm grateful to hear a child laugh. I'm grateful that today when a car cut me off, I laughed instead of cursing.

Scriptures at a Glance

"Then they cried to the Lord in their trouble, and He saved them from their distress.

•••

He sent forth His word and healed them; He rescued them from the grave" (Psalm 107:19-20).

•••

"For Your sake we are being put to death all day long; we were considered as sheep to be slaughtered. But in all these things we overwhelmingly conquer through Him who loved us. For I am convinced that neither death, nor life, nor angels, nor principalities, nor things present, nor things to come, nor powers, nor height, nor depth, nor any other created thing, will be able to separate us from the love of God, which is in Jesus Christ our Lord" (Romans 8:36-39 NASB).

"Have I not commanded you? Be strong and courageous. Do not be terrified; do not be discouraged, for the Lord your God will be with you wherever you go" (Joshua 1:9).

•••

"For I know the plans I have for you," declares the Lord, "plans to prosper you and not to harm you, plans to give you hope and a future" (Jeremiah 29:11).

•••

"Be still and know that I am God" (Psalm 46:10a).

•••

"Never will I leave you; never will I forsake you" (Hebrews 13:5b).

•••

"Until now you have not asked for anything in my name. Ask and you will receive, and your joy will be complete" (John 16:24).

•••

"Bearing with one another, and forgiving one another, whoever has a complaint against anyone, just as the Lord forgave you, so also should you" (Colossians 3:13 NASB).

•••

"For God did not give us a spirit of timidity, but a spirit of power, of love and of self-discipline" (2 Timothy 1:7).

"Do not be anxious about anything, but in everything, by prayer and petition, with thanksgiving, present your requests to God. And the peace of God, which transcends all understanding, will guard your hearts and your minds in Christ Jesus" (Philippians 4:6–7).

•••

"Do not forsake wisdom, and she will protect you; love her, and she will watch over you" (Proverbs 4:6).

•••

"He will cover you with His feathers, and under His wings you will find refuge; His faithfulness will be your shield and rampart" (Psalm 91:4).

•••

"I can do everything through Him who gives me strength" (Philippians 4:13).

•••

"The wise woman builds her house, but the foolish pulls it down with her hands" (Proverbs 14:1 NKJV).

•••

"So I say to you, ask, and it will be given to you; seek, and you will find; knock, and it will be opened to you" (Matthew 7:7 NASB).

"But those who hope in the Lord will renew their strength. They will soar on wings like eagles; they will run and not grow weary, they will walk and not be faint" (Isaiah 40:31).

•••

"Do everything without complaining or arguing" (Philippians 2:14).

•••

"Trust in the Lord with all your heart and do not lean on your own understanding; in all your ways acknowledge Him, and He will make your paths straight" (Proverbs 3:5-6).

•••

"If we confess our sins, He is faithful and just and will forgive us our sins and purify us from all unrighteousness" (1 John 1:9).

•••

"Devote yourselves to prayer, being watchful and thankful" (Colossians 4:2).

•••

"For nothing is impossible with God" (Luke 1:37).

Tools

Exercise: Forgiveness Visualization

You may read through each step and do the exercise by memory, have someone read the exercise aloud to you, or listen to a recording of it in your own voice. Go slowly and give yourself the opportunity to visualize and feel your emotions. It may take more than once to fully relax, but you should feel some relief each time you do this exercise.

1. Relax. Close your eyes and take a few deep, cleansing breaths. Now allow the person you need to forgive right now to come into your mind.

2. Visualize this person standing about 10 feet away from you and with a cord connecting the two of you.

3. Invite God to join you. Believe that God has your greatest interest at heart and God is here to protect, love and support you through this process.

4. Take your time and express what you are thinking and how you are feeling to this person who has hurt you. Tell them everything that is on your mind and in your heart.

5. When you are finished, you may find that the person would like to say something to you. Allow them to express themselves. You may want to respond and let the dialogue continue. (Remember this is a visualization, and it is an internal dialogue.)

6. When you feel you are ready to release the person who has hurt you, notice God has given you a pair of golden scissors. You may ask God to assist you in severing the connection with this person. Tell them you are now ready to release the cords that bind you. Tell them you are ready to forgive them. Proclaim you are ready to be free. (At this step, I also actively prayed for the other person and asked God to take over the situation and bless each of us.)

7. Envision yourself severing the connection you have with this person.

8. After the cord has been cut, imagine surrounding yourself with a circle of light or a protective irides-

cent bubble. You are now establishing new boundaries and are no longer a victim of this person. If you think of or see this person, you will feel safe and whole. Bless them on their path and know you are now free, supported and blessed on your path.

Tools

Exercise: Signs of Depression

In *When It's More Than Just the Blues*, by Dean Anderson (http://www.sparkpeople.com/resource/wellness_articles.asp?id=757), a behavioral psychology expert, he states the following:

It isn't always easy to tell when normal reactions to difficult situations (grief, sadness, etc.) have crossed the line towards clinical depression and need treatment. However, the number of signs or symptoms you are experiencing, along with the duration and frequency you have them are all important. If you have experienced five or more of the following symptoms (including one of the first two listed) nearly every day for two weeks or more, this warrants a visit to your doctor for evaluation:

1. Loss of interest in things you normally enjoy

2. Feeling down, depressed, or hopeless

3. Thoughts of death or suicide

4. Feeling worthless or guilty

5. Problems falling asleep, staying asleep, waking too early, or sleeping too much

6. Unexplained decrease or increase in appetite, resulting in weight gain or loss within the last month.

7. Trouble thinking, concentrating, remembering, and making decisions

8. Extreme tiredness or lack of energy that interferes with your ability to work or take care of your daily responsibilities

9. Feeling restless, unable to sit still, or abnormally slow when moving

Take a look at the list and consider if you need a mental health evaluation from a licensed medical professional.

Recommended Reading

Manifesting Love From the Inside Out. Tammi Baliszewski, PhD. Eagle, Idaho: Expanding Heart Publishing, 2009.

Healed & Set Free...from Lingering Hurts. Tammy Brown. Idaho Falls, Idaho: Calvary Chapel of Idaho Falls, 2000.

Shrink Yourself: Break Free from Emotional Eating Forever! Roger Gould, MD. Hoboken, New Jersey: John Wiley & Sons, Inc., 2007.

Boundaries: When to Say Yes, When to Say No, To Take Control of Your Life. Dr. Henry Cloud and Dr. John Townsend. Grand Rapids, Michigan: Zondervan, 1992.

Getting Past Your Past: Take Control of Your Life with Self-Help Techniques from EMDR Therapy. Francine Shapiro, PhD. New York: Rodale, Inc., 2012.

Acknowledgments

Cole, what a gift you are in my life. It is a pleasure to be your mom. I look forward to developing a collaborative and inspiring relationship that enriches both of our lives. I love watching how you are developing your gifts and learning how to share them. The way you love is simply amazing!

Mom, thank you for showing me what a hard working and compassionate woman looks like. Thank you for loving me unconditionally. I believe that you have taught me well.

I miss you, Dad! I miss your strong hands that easily fix things, your dry sense of humor, and the words, "I love you," that I feel so fortunate to have heard from my earthly father. I was a lucky girl. Thank you for teaching me to love the outdoors and the wonderful creatures in it.

Mark, my brother and hero! Thank you for sharing your creative gift of design to the world and loving your family with deep compassion and commitment.

Diane, my sister and friend. You are an incredibly strong and talented woman. You have created a great life for yourself and your family.

My nieces: Teal, Erika, Sophia, Jennifer, and Debrah—simply incredible women each and every one of you. Teal, I can't wait to see your designs on the runway! Erika, you outstand the world everyday with your many facets of faces and the human expression. Sophia, I loved our time together and cannot wait to see the many talents you will share with others. Jennifer and Debrah, two beautiful women I feel blessed to call family. Andrea, you are not forgotten.

Lizzie, thank you for the amazing way you love all the people in your life, especially our family.

Christa, my dear, radiant friend. Wherever you are, the sun shines a little brighter. Your compassion, humor, and collaboration are inspiring.

Randi, my sweet childhood friend. You are an earthly angel who inspires women to be the best they can be.

Sweet Amber, you are full of warmth and compassion. It is truly wonderful seeing you raise such a remarkable daughter.

Ann C., a dear and heartfelt friend who loves her family, friends, and patients with passion and warmth. I am so grateful that I may call you friend.

Tammy B, your inspiring guidance to explore my creative gifts has been an adventure. Thank you, thank you, thank you. The wealth of knowledge you have and the willingness to share with others are vibrant and colorful as the beautiful mandalas you paint.

Lisa M., Carrie, Berta, Suzanne, Judy, and Tod, thank you for your love on this journey called life. I love you all. Wish our paths crossed more often.

The entire team at Aloha Publishing of incredible professionals guiding and teaching me: Maryanna Young, you are an amazing leader, encouraging this new writer along this exciting path. I feel like I received an incredible gift in 2012 when I met you. Kim, a patient, diligent and fabulous editor. Thank you for taking my writing and making it shine. You are truly gifted. Kelly Cope, your promotional guidance is super extraordinary. Thanks from the bottom of my heart!

Cari and Amy, thank you for creating a cover that was better than what I initially envisioned.

Shiloh, I didn't even know a book had an interior designer. You blow me away with your great talents.

Authors in the Summer Workshop: Joel, Brandon, Angela, and Rob, I loved Thursdays because of all of you. I cannot wait to see your books in readers' hands and seeing the smiles on their faces. You have changed my life forever!

Jim L., what a dear friend. I hope this encourages you to write and share your stories.

Kristal, my childhood friend and sister from a different mother. Your humorous tilt on life keeps smiles on all our faces.

Jim K., a counselor who taught me *so* many things. You taught me to stretch and that all things are possible—not to be limited to rules.

Ann A., thank you for the creative ways in re-creating my business and my goals. You believed in me when I didn't. Thank you in sharing the wonderful person you are.

Barb, my first editor. I love the fresh way you look at things and the energy in which you live life. You amaze me!

Susie, a smile comes across my face when I think of you and our escapades.

Barb B., thank you for sharing who you are. I appreciate our friendship.

Dr. Eric, thanks for being a wonderful healing doctor to all our family.

Keith, your creative mind, passion and ability to make something out of nothing are nothing short of amazing. I hope to see the gift you made in every little leaguers backyard some day.

To others whom I am forever thankful for and have been enriched by: Ann A. Lori, Deanna, Polly, Annette, Dawn, Jim V., Renee, Jennifer, J.D., Anjanette, Jerry, Betty, Dorinda, Tami, Donise, Bob, Vada, Jim, Shirley, Steve, Laurie and Virgina.

To all the amazing Keller Williams coaches, colleagues, mentors and friends: You develop yourselves to be the best you can be and inspire others to do the same – what a wonderful place to be a part of everyday!

To all my clients – You have blessed my life in knowing and serving you.

There are so many people whom I could thank for their love and support and gracing my life with their presence.

You know who you are, and I thank you from the bottom of my heart.

Jesus, thank You for walking this earth and showing us a better way to live and to love! I desire to love the way You did!

About the Author

Michele de Reus is a native Idahoan residing in Boise. After receiving her Bachelors in Business Administration at Boise State University and studying abroad in Avignon, France for a term, she came home and married her college sweetheart.

Life was going well, her career was taking off when she was blindsided to face infidelity and depression. Not knowing where to turn, she voraciously read and sought counseling. Through her experience, she found some misguided information, only leaving her further feeling dark and shallow. Her self confidence and self worth were severely damaged. Luckily, instead of throwing out her spiritual connection, she embraced it. Her perseverance to finding truth and having a loving support system of family, friends and professionals was the grace transformation in her life.

Encouraged by a life coach in 2011 to consider writing to share and help others, she courageously stepped in and is one of the contributing authors in the anthology "Change One Belief", published in the summer of 2012 and her first book "Daring to Choose". She gives helpful, proven strategies that have helped her and other women in some of their darkest days to get you on the path of living life with joy, hope, and inspiration. It is her genuine desire to help women know that they are loved by God, know they are worthy, and to be encouraged to develop their gifts and share them with the world.

In the professional arena, she is an Associate Broker, and has worked in the real estate industry since 2003. She is currently on the board of the local chapter of Women's Council of Realtors. Whether it is working with clients on their real estate needs or teaching indoor cycling at the local gym, she focuses on her personal and professional motto, "In all you do, create an environment for success."

Her greatest joy in life has been to raise her only son and watch him begin his adult adventures. She too is an adventurer of life so you might see her traveling with friends and family, skiing somewhere in the Northwest, or hiking the Boise foothills. She is passionate in being an advocate of women who want to step up and not be a victim to their circumstance but to rise above it!